Toilet-bound Hanako-Kun

5

Contents

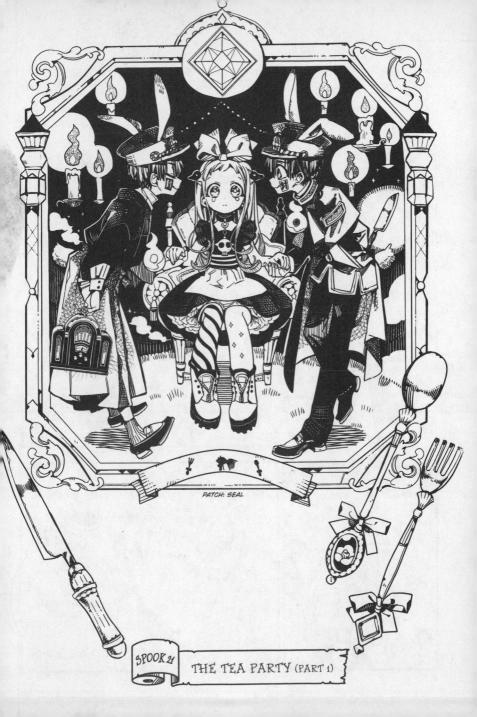

PATCH: SEAL

SPOOK 21

THE TEA PARTY (PART 1)

PLAYAAA...

BUT, COME ON! HE'S A TOTAL HOTTIE!

AND THIS HAS NEVER HAPPENED TO ME BEFORE!!

IT MIGHT NEVER HAPPEN AGAIN!!

HNGH...!

...I DIDN'T THINK. I JUST FOLLOWED HIM...

HMM?

SENPAI, WHO...?

UM...

BUT... WHAT IN THE WORLD COULD HE WANT WITH ME?

ヘ○ラ BLAH

AND, FYI, I'M ALWAYS ON THE HUNT FOR A GIRL-FRIEND! ☆

MY HOBBIES INCLUDE FISHING AND KARAOKE.

HIGH SCHOOL DIVISION, SECOND-YEAR, CLASS B.

ヘ○ラ BLAH

ヘ○ラ BLAH

OH, ME?

I'M NATSUHIKO HYUUGA!

CALL ME NATSUHIKO-SENPAI! ♡

C'MON, CALL ME NATSUHIKO-SENPAI! ♥

OH! LET'S TRADE NUMBERS!

HYUUGA-SENPAI...

THIS IS THE FIRST TIME WE'VE TALKED, ISN'T IT?

HMM? OH, THERE'S SOMEONE WHO WANTS TO MEET YOU!

TRADING CONTACT INFO...

SOME-ONE WHO WANTS TO MEET ME...?

UM... WHY DO YOU WANT TO TALK TO ME, SENPAI...?

PLEASE

SPECIAL? OH, DO GO ON...

ER.

UM...

I DUNNO. MAYBE BECAUSE... YOU'RE SUCH A SPECIAL GIRL?

BUT WHY ME?

6

HMM?

WHY ARE YOU HOLDING A GOLDFISH BOWL?

......

FIDGET
T=
U

I'M SURE I HAVE NO IDEA...

I...

PAT
PAT

SPLISH
SPLISH

WHY DO YOU THIIINK ...?

......!!!!

HA-HA!

YOINK

WHAT IS THIS? WHAT'S GOING ON!?

WHY!?

FLOP

FLOP

FLOP

NENE TURNS INTO A FISH WHEN WET!

GOTCHA! ♥

AAAAH...

NOPE, STILL ALIVE...

SHE DIED.

REST IN PEACE.

ホ
チャ
SPLISH

...

AAAAAAAAAAAAA...

FLOP

キュゥ...

NNGH...

THERE'S WATER AT MY FEET!!!

WHICH MEANS THIS IS...

SPLASH
ばしゃ

DESSERTS ...?

SOMETHING SMELLS REALLY GOOD...

...A BOUNDARY...?

ARE YOU AWAKE?

I TOLD THEM TO BE GENTLE WITH YOU...

...BUT THOSE BOYS NEVER LISTEN.

OH!

YOU'RE...!

JUST WHO...

ゴクリ
GULP

I AM NOT DATING HIM.

...ARE THESE PEOPLE...!?

SORRY

YES, MA'AM.

THEY SURE DO GET ALONG!

LET'S START OVER.

PLEASED TO MEET YOU, NENE YASHIRO-SAN.

I'M VERY SORRY FOR NOT PAYING MY RESPECTS SOONER.

HUH?

HE'S A BIT CHILDISH...

...BUT SURPRISINGLY RELIABLE.

ぽと
PLOP

MY FATE HAS BEEN TIED TO THIS BOY'S.

HE DESERVES ABOUT AS MUCH ATTENTION AS THE AIR.

GLINT
キリッ

IS... IS THAT SO...?

OH...

WHAT ABOUT NATSUHIKO-SENPAI?

GLANCE
チラ

YOU SEE...

...YOU AND I...WE'RE IN THE SAME POSITION.

I'VE BEEN WANTING TO TALK TO YOU.

DON'T YOU?

I THINK WE COULD BE GOOD FRIENDS.

ACK!

NOW THAT I SEE HER UP CLOSE, SHE'S SO PRETTY...

LIKE A DOLL...

WOW...

SHE'S BOUND TO A SUPER-NATURAL...

YOU HAVE TO THINK!

KEEP IT TOGETHER, NENE!

YOU CAN'T LET YOUR GUARD DOWN JUST BECAUSE SHE'S A BABE!

SHAKE
SHAKE

EVEN IF SHE REALLY IS JUST LIKE ME...

...WHAT ARE THEY ALL DOING HERE?

GRIT

I...

I WON'T LET THEM FOOL ME!

THAT'S DEFINITELY, WELL, FISHY!

AND THEY SEEMED TO KNOW THAT I TURN INTO A FISH WHEN I GET WET...

17

GULP ぐび

GULP ぐび

GULP ぐび

IT'S TRUE!

HANAKO-KUN IS LIKE THAT ALL THE TIME, AND I JUST DON'T KNOW WHAT TO DO ABOUT IT...!

THIS TEA IS SO DELICIOUS...

THIRTY MINUTES LATER

THAT SOUNDS ROUGH...

IT'S WHITE PEACH INFUSED GREEN TEA. MAKE SURE TO HAVE PLENTY.

SOB

LIKE, HIS ATTITUDE WILL SUDDENLY FLIP FOR THE MOST UNPREDICTABLE REASONS!

I CAN'T MAKE SENSE OF HIM......

RADISH?

?

AND I AM NOT A RADISH!!

BANG だ

FLINCH ん

HE'S SO INCONSIDERATE!

AND WHAT'S MORE, HE KEEPS SAYING THESE WEIRD, CRYPTIC THINGS...

PLUS, HE SEXUALLY HARASSES ME.

AWWW, YOU THINK SO?

MOST PEOPLE WOULD.

GET OFF.

GLOMP

I HAVE IT PRETTY HARD TOO.

HE NEVER LISTENS TO ME, HIS ACTIONS MAKE NO SENSE...

...AND HE HAS NO SENSE OF PERSONAL SPACE.

I CAN'T SAY I DON'T KNOW HOW YOU FEEL.

SIGH...

...

UM.

MEOW!

SO I'VE DECIDED TO THINK OF HIM MORE AS A CAT THAN A PERSON.

...BUT THERE'S NOTHING I CAN DO ABOUT IT.

MEOW!

HAAH...

A CAT...

GULP

THAT BOY...

YOU MEAN ME?

20

TH-TH-THAT STARTLED ME...

PEEL

STOP THAT.

BADUM

BADUM! BADUM!

AND WAIT...

THIS TEA IS DELICIOUS!

THIRTY MINUTES

I WON'T BE FOOLED!!

I'M SO STUPID! STUPID!!

AFTER I JUST TOLD MYSELF TO BE ON MY GUARD!

I LET MYSELF GET WRAPPED UP IN GIRL TALK...!!

NOOOOOO!

CLANG

LOVE & HARMONY

BUT COME ON! I'VE NEVER BEEN ABLE TO TALK TO ANOTHER GIRL ABOUT HANAKO-KUN BEFORE!

I WAS JUST SO HAPPY...

GLANCE

BUT THEY DRAGGED ME HERE AGAINST MY WILL.

WAS IT REALLY JUST SO WE COULD TALK...?

...THEY DON'T REALLY LOOK LIKE BAD PEOPLE.

WHEN YOU TOUCH A GIRL, YOU HAVE TO MAKE IT MORE NATURAL, GENTLER...

BUT THEY'RE SO MUCH MORE NORMAL THAN I EXPECTED... I MEAN...

YOU WANNA KISS ME, SAKURA?

NO.

NNNGH...

IN THAT CASE, I WISH THEY WOULD'VE JUST BROUGHT ME HERE LIKE NORMAL...

SAKURA.

......

23

SIGH...

GUESS WHAT!? WHEN I DISOBEY HANAKO-KUN, HE IMMEDIATELY THREATENS TO TURN ME INTO A FISH...

I KNOW THE FEELING.

...WE CAN'T DISOBEY OUR MASTERS, NO MATTER HOW MUCH WE HATE THEIR ORDERS.

SO LONG AS WE'RE BOUND TO THEM...

I KNOW, RIGHT!?

WE BOTH HAVE OUR HARDSHIPS.

YES.

AND SO I'M SURE...

CLASP
がしっ

YOU TOO, NANAMINE-SENPAI?

...YOU'LL UNDER-STAND.

LOOM

I REALLY DIDN'T WANT TO DO THIS.

LET ME GO!!

I WOULD SAVE YOU IF I COULD.

BUT I CAN'T DISOBEY HIM.

I'M SORRY.

IN A WORD, I GUESS WE'RE RIVALS? ARCH-NEMESES?

WELL, WHATEVER. ANYWAY.

AMANE AND I ARE, LIKE, POLAR OPPOSITES, Y'KNOW?

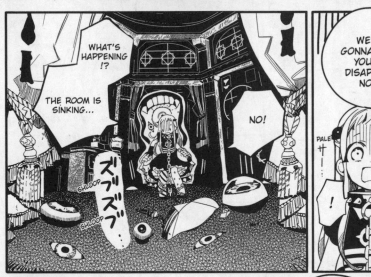

WHAT'S HAPPENING!?

THE ROOM IS SINKING...

NO!

SHLOOP

SHLOOP

WE'RE GONNA NEED YOU TO DISAPPEAR NOW.

PALE

!

CREAK

BYE-BYE!

Y-Y-YOU'RE KIDDING, RIGHT!?

WAIT...

I'M GLAD I COULD TALK TO YOU ONCE BEFORE THE END.

FAREWELL.

29

SHE'S ODDLY HARD ON ME, I GUESS? LIKE...SHE'S ESPECIALLY ROUGH WITH ME.

YEAAAH... SHE'S LIKE THIS SOME- TIMES.

YOU'RE ON THEIR SIDE, AREN'T YOU!?

NATSUHIKO- SENPAI!?

WHY!?

NO, THAT DOESN'T MAKE ANY SENSE AT ALL.

HEH...

SPECIAL TREATMENT... JUST FOR ME...

COULD IT BE LOVE...?

ANYWAY...

...ARE YOU ONE OF THOSE PEOPLE WHO'RE OKAY WITH DYING?

WE HAVE TO DO SOMETHING, OR EVERYTHING'S GONNA SINK...

WH-WH-WH-WHAT DO WE DO!?

R-R-R-RIGHT, Y-Y-Y-YEAH!

BECAUSE IF YOU'RE NOT, I'M PRETTY SURE THIS ISN'T AN IDEAL SITUATION.

SPLOOP

どっぷり…

ばた
FLAIL

ANYWAY, I HAVE TO GRAB ONTO SOMETHING...

ばた
FLAIL

I... I CAN'T MOVE!?

S-SOME-BODY!

HELP!

SOFF

!!

WARGH!

SPLISH

ばちゃん

WHENEVER I'M IN DANGER...

...HANAKO-KUN HAS ALWAYS COME TO MY RESCUE.

WHENEVER I'M IN TROUBLE...

...EY.

HEEEY!

WAKE UUUP...!

I'M SURE...

I'M SURE HANAKO-KUN WILL SAVE ME.

SO I'M SURE I'LL MAKE IT THROUGH THIS.

SPOOK 22   THE TEA PARTY (PART 2)

ACK!

NO, NO!! NATSUHIKO-SENPAI IS IN LEAGUE WITH THE PEOPLE WHO WANT TO ERASE ME!!

SCARY PEOPLE

THOUGH IT DOESN'T SEEM LIKE THEY'RE REALLY TRYING TO KILL ME...

I SHOULD HAVE LET HIM KISS ME!

WHAT HAVE I DONE? HOW COULD I WASTE THAT GOLDEN OPPORTUNITY....!?

SLUMP

GULP

N-NOTHING!

WHAT'S WRONG? NENE-CHAN?

THIS IS MORE DISAPPOINTING THAN EXPECTED...

THINK OF HIM AS AIR.

EXAMPLES OF NOT QUITE RIGHT

AND NATSUHIKO-SENPAI IS HOT... BUT SOMETHING'S NOT QUITE RIGHT ABOUT HIM...

IS THIS...

ANYWAY, WHAT HAPPENED TO US?

THE ROOM SANK, AND...

THERE ARE SO MANY DOORS...

LOTS OF MOKKE-CHAN TOO.

...A BOUNDARY TOO...?

BUT THERE'S NO WATER...

Not quite a Boundary, I'd say.

AH!

HEY!! THAT VOICE...

FLOWER HAL

38

Over here.

TEP TEP て て て TEP

WHERE ARE YOU? ARE YOU CLOSE BY?

GLANCE キ ョ ロ

GLANCE キ ョ ロ

IS THAT YOU, HANAKO-KUN?

Hello, Yashiro.

HOPPITY ピ ョ ッ コ ン

HEH...

...and you're off after some hot guy or supernatural.

I take my eyes off you for one second...

URK...

I TRICKED HER!

ピ カ

DIIING

HOT GUY

Yashiro, you got tricked again, huh?

And if you're there, that means...

YES.

A RADIO...?

WOW...

HNNGH!

IT'S SUCH A HANDFUL, HAVING AN ASSISTANT LIKE YOU.

HANAKO-KUUUUN...!

TEARY

YOU HAVE ANYTHING TO SAY TO ME?

THEY KIDNAPPED ME!

I WAS AT A TEA PARTY!

AND I MEANT TO BE CAREFUL, BUT—!

WAAAH!

WAAAH!

Very good.

I'M SORRY I LET THEM TRICK ME.

THE DESSERTS WERE SO YUMMY, I JUST... I JUST...

...isn't the Near Shore, the Far Shore, or a Boundary...

It's a place that's nowhere.

Where you are right now...

MM-HMM.

NOWHERE...?

NOW THEN.

I DON'T KNOW HOW LONG THIS TRANSMISSION WILL LAST, SO I'LL MAKE THIS SHORT.

SO I'M GOING TO NEED YOU TO WORK AT THIS TOO.

...BUT THAT PLACE IS JUST SO BIG.

I CAN USE OUR BOND TO HELP HAKUJOUDAI FIND YOU.

I WANT TO SAVE YOU SOMEHOW...

YUP.

IT'S NOWHERE, BUT EVERYWHERE, AND IT CAN TAKE YOU ANYWHERE...

IT'S AN ANNOYING SORT OF PLACE LIKE THAT.

1964
2013
1886
1921
2009
775

WHAT SHOULD I DO?

RIGHT.

You see a lot of doors, right?

All of those doors...

...lead to a different place in a different world.

I want you to look for it on your end...

...and open it up for me.

WAY HOME

There should be a door somewhere that leads to the world you came from.

BUT SOME OF THEM'LL LEAD TO DANGEROUS PLACES.

DOORS THAT LOOK FAMILIAR.

SO YOU'LL HAVE TO BE CARE- FUL...

UM... SO...

...I JUST HAVE TO OPEN DOORS?

I LOST THE CONNECTION...

CLICK ブツン

...Good lu...

...Uh-oh.

Time's ...

ガ KRNK

ガ" KRR

ピ KRR

HANAKO-KUN!?

KZH

KZH

KZH

Really, I...so... but...

FINISHED?

IF ONE OF THE SEVEN MYSTERIES SAYS SO, IT MUST BE THE RIGHT THING TO DO.

DOORS THAT LOOK FAMILIAR, HUH...?

HMMM...

YES... HE SAID TO OPEN DOORS THAT LOOK FAMILIAR.

IS THIS STALL FREE...?

JUST LEAVE IT TO NATSUHIKO-SENPAIII...!

JUST KIDDING!

ガチャッ KACHAK

I'LL BE FIIINE!

AND HE SAID TO BE CAREFUL BECAUSE SOME OF THEM LEAD TO DANGEROUS PLACES!

OH!

LIKE THIS ONE?

コン コン コン KNOCK KNOCK KNOCK

OCCUPIED.

ばあ BOING

EEK!

...YEAH.

LET'S JUST... GO AHEAD AND PRETEND THAT DIDN'T HAPPEN.

ドキ BADUM
ドキ BADUM
ドキ BADUM
ドキ
ドキ BADUM
ドキ BADUM

パタン SHUT

GLANCE チラ

WHOOSH
どおお

THAT BEING THE CASE, UNO MÁS!

WAAAAH! WAIT!

!?

パカッ

POP

2ND DOOR

GLUB
オォォ

BURBLE
ボコォォォ

BURBLE
ボコッ

THIRD TIME'S THE CHARM!

パカッ

POP

3RD DOOR

ROAR
ゴォッ

FZH
ジュッ

THIS ONE'S GOTTA WORK!

パカッ

POP

4TH DOOR

YES, LET'S.

PLEASE.

LET'S PROCEED WITH CAUTION.

...I GOT AN IDEA.

SHUT バタン

IT'S JUST— WHEN I'M WITH A CUTE GIRL, I FEEL LIKE I NEED TO SHOW OFF...!

RIGHT...

HA HA!

MAN... SORRY 'BOUT THAT.

HMMM?

UM...

...

WELL, NATSUHIKO-SENPAI'S ANTICS ARE HELPING ME KEEP MY MIND OFF THINGS AT LEAST, BUT...

HE'S NOT SORRY AT ALL...

AIEEEE!

O WOW...

PEEL ペリ

HEH...

...THIS MIGHT REALLY BE... A TRIAL OF LOVE.

AH.

SLAM

OH NO, OH NO, OH NO!

DRAG DRAG DRAG

AAAAAAH!

GOOD LUCK.

N— NENE-CHAN...

ギイイ

GREEEAK

GRAB

ガッ

し…ん
HUSH

SLAM

I CANNOT LET NATSUHIKO-SENPAI'S SACRIFICE BE IN VAIN...

★ FAREWELL......!!!

HE'S DEAD?

HE'S DEAD.

I MUST GO ON...

ACTUALLY, I FEEL LIKE NATSUHIKO-SENPAI'S GONNA BE FINE.

IT'S JUST A HUNCH, THOUGH.

たたた... TEP TEP TEP TEP

IF ONLY I HAD SOMETHING TO GO ON.

SOME SORT OF CLUE...

BUT WHAT DO I DO?

IT REALLY WOULDN'T BE SAFE TO OPEN DOORS AT RANDOM LIKE NATSUHIKO-SENPAI WAS DOING...

HMMM

HMM?

WHISPER

WHISPER WHISPER

VOICES...OR SOUNDS...?

IT'S COMING FROM THE OTHER SIDE OF THE DOOR...

CLING

AH!

THIS MUSIC!

HUM HUM HUM HUM HUM

I COULDN'T TELL BEFORE, BECAUSE NATSUHIKO-SENPAI WAS TALKING.

GYAAAH!

BLAH BLAH BLAH BLAH BLAH

POP
パカッ

GYAAAH!

パタン…
SLAM

I'VE HEARD IT BEFORE... I KNOW THIS SOUND...

WHERE IS IT COMING FROM!?

TURN
ばっ

WRONG DOOR...

I WAS SURE I RECOGNIZED THAT MUSIC...

ぴょ
HOP
ぴょ
HOP
ぴょ
HOP

THIS IS...

I SHOULD GO AROUND BEHIND IT?

HUH? WHAT?

It is now
five thirty.

GLINT

I...

WH...

I KNEW I'D HEARD THAT MUSIC BEFORE...

IT'S THE EVENING ANNOUNCE-MENT!

I DID IT!

"CRASH"?

HANAKO-KUN!?

DRIP

じわ…

HANAKO-KUN...

THAT LOOKS PAINFUL... WHAT HAPPENED?

FRET
オロ

オロ
FRET

た っ
TEP

JOLT
ビク

ARE YOU HURT!?

SIGN: GIRLS' TOILET

女子便所

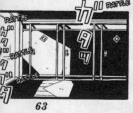

RATTLE

ガタ
ガタ
ガタ

RATTLE

RATTLE

RATTLE

DIIING

DAAANG

DOOONG

DOOONG

キーンコーンコーン

カーンコーンコーン

HANAKO-
KUN...

HUH?

EXCUSE ME
A SECOND.

WHAT STRANGE
CLOTHES YOU'RE
WEARING!

'CLÁAÁNG'
ガーン...

"STRANGE"
...

EEK!

WHAT?

WHAT'S WRONG!?

CALM DOWN, CALM DOWN.

SQUEEZE

THIS IS MORE MY STYLE.

THERE WE GO!

HEE HEE!

POP

ONE...

TWO...

THREE...

BUT YOU SEE...

...THERE ARE GUARDS WATCHING OVER THE BIG CLOCK.

THEY ARE THE THREE CLOCK KEEPERS, WHO REPRESENT PAST, PRESENT, AND FUTURE.

...THE THREE CLOCK KEEPERS WILL STEAL THE TIME FROM THAT PERSON'S LIFE...!

IF ANYONE TOUCHES THE CLOCK WITHOUT THEIR PERMISSION...

IT'S A PRETTY POPULAR RUMOR THESE DAYS! ❤

SO THERE YOU HAVE IT!

DIIING
キーン

DAAANG
カーン

DOOONG
コーン

DOOONG
コーン

MURMUR
ガヤ

MURMUR
ガヤ

70

IT'S JUST...

I...

OH, I'M SORRY.

WHAT IS IT?

NENE-CHAN.

......

TICK カチ TOCK コチ

TICK カチ TOCK コチ

?

I HAVE SOMETHING I HAVE TO TELL YOU, NENE-CHAN...

TICK カチ TOCK コチ TICK カチ TOCK コチ TICK カチ TOCK コチ TICK カチ

I...

TICK カチ TOCK コチ TICK カチ TOCK コチ

ACTUALLY, I...

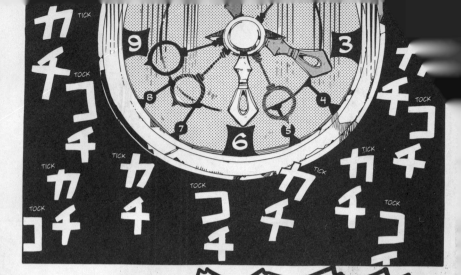

WAAAAAAAAAAAHH!!

WAS THAT FROM OUR CLASS...?

WH-WHAT!?

MURMUR

MURMUR

!!

OH...

WHAT'S WRONG!?

TEP

...WH—

THIS MORNING

IT WAS NORMAL THIS MORNING.

WHY THE SUDDEN GROWTH SPURT...?

ISN'T THIS OUR CLASS'S POTTED PLANT...?

IT'S SO BIG NOW!

THIS TREE...

RUSTLE

IT'S ALMOST LIKE...

SIGN: GIRLS' TOILET

女子便所

KOU-KUN.

HANA-KOOOO!!!

SKIIID

STOMP STOMP

GRAB

WAH!

····

KOU-KUN, THIS IS THE GIRLS' RESTROOM. TECHNICALLY.

TAG: TRAFFIC-SAFETY CHARM

THEY... THEY...

SENPAI! YES— YES, IT DID.

YOU MEAN SOMETHING HAPPENED IN YOUR CLASS TOO, KOU-KUN?

SHAKE

WAAAGH!

FLOP

SHAKE

YOU GOTTA HELP!!

SATOU AND YOKOO FROM MY CLASS, THEY'RE—!

SHAKE

THEY'VE TURNED INTO OLD MEN!!!

BEFORE

AFTER

どーーん
DUDUUUN

SENSEI SAID...THERE MUST HAVE BEEN SOME SUSPICIOUS CHARACTERS PLAYING PRANKS ON OUR CLASSROOM.

BUT DO YOU THINK IT'S...?

THEY'RE SURPRISINGLY CHILL ABOUT IT.

THAT IS BAD...

SOMEONE WILL PAY... THEY'RE ONLY FOURTEEN!!

WHEN FOURTH PERIOD WAS OVER, THEY HAD SUDDENLY CHANGED...

GRIT

OLD MAN PARTY

YUP.

THIS IS THE WORK OF A SUPERNATURAL!

BLUNT

けろり

MM-HMM!

SATOU!! YOKOO!!

NOOOO!

THE BOUNDARIES ARE BIG PLACES.

BUT THERE AREN'T A WHOLE LOT OF SUPER-NATURALS WHO CAN DO SOMETHING LIKE THIS.

THAT REMINDS ME, AOI WAS SAYING...

...THERE'S A MYSTERIOUS OLD CLOCK AND THREE CLOCK KEEPERS.

OH, YOU'VE HEARD OF IT. THAT SAVES US TIME.

THE SEVEN MYSTERIES ...

ODDS ARE...

...ONE OF THE SEVEN MYSTERIES IS INVOLVED IN THIS.

MM-HMM!

!

SKIIID

KOU-KUN.

HANA-KOOOO!!!

JOLT

GRAB

WAH!

....

STOMP

STOMP

KOU-KUN, THIS IS THE GIRLS' RESTROOM. TECHNICALLY.

TAG: TRAFFIC-SAFETY CHARM

THEY... THEY...

SENPAI! YES— YES, IT DID.

FLOP

YOU MEAN SOMETHING HAPPENED IN YOUR CLASS TOO, KOU-KUN?

WAAAGH!

SHAKE

SHAKE

SHAKE

SHAKE

YOU GOTTA HELP!!

SATOU AND YOKOO FROM MY CLASS, THEY'RE—!

......

...WHAT?

I SAID...

I DON'T KNOW.

DUNNO!

HMM...

WHERE IS THAT SUPER-NATURAL!?

SO, HANAKO!

OH! A BUTTER-FLY!

MAYBE IT COMES FROM BEING GUARDIANS, BUT THEY CAN BE A LITTLE PRUDISH...

YEAH... IT'S JUST, No. 1...

ギギギ ギリリリ

STRANGLE STRANGLE STRANGLE STRANGLE

AREN'T YOU SUPPOSED TO BE THE LEADER OF THE SEVEN MYSTERIES !!?

YOU CAN CONTROL TIME!? THAT'S AWESOME!

I'LL NEVER FORGET THE FIRST TIME WE MET...

AND THE THIRD MOVES TIME FORWARD.

ALLLLL RIGHT!!

LET'S GO SOCK IT TO 'IM! RIGHT NOW!!

AND I'LL HELP!

'COS I'M HANAKO-KUN'S ASSISTANT!!

AND SATOU AND YOKOO...

SO MY CLASS-ROOM...

FROM WHAT YOU'VE SAID, IT WAS THE THIRD KEEPER, NO DOUBT ABOUT IT.

ooo

SCHOOL
MYSTERY
No. 1—

THE
THREE CLOCK
KEEPERS.

THE
THREE OF
THEM...

...EACH
HAVE THEIR
OWN POWER
TO CONTROL
TIME.

THE
SECOND
STOPS
TIME.

THE
FIRST CAN
TURN BACK
TIME.

AND THEN THEY SAID THEY NEVER WANTED TO SEE ME AGAIN.

WOULDN'T EVEN TELL ME WHERE THEIR BOUNDARY WAS.

TEE HEE!

YOU...

KOU

YOU DAMN PERVERT!!

YOU CAN DO ALL THE PERVY STUFF YOU WANT!!!

STEAM

I SAID I WOULDN'T!!

BUT, YOU COULD DO IT AS MUCH AS YOU WANTED...!?

I WON'T SPELL IT OUT FOR YOU, BUT...

UGH, BOYS...

I WOULD NOT!

LIKE YOU WOULDN'T DO ANYTHING PERVERTED IF YOU COULD CONTROL TIME...!?

WHAT...?

I DON'T BELIEVE THAT.

THE MIDDLE ONE OF THE THREE CLOCK KEEPERS...

I MIGHT'VE HEARD JUST ONE THING.

OH, BUT!

SO... YOU'RE NO BETTER OFF THAN WE ARE, HANAKO-KUN?

YOU DON'T KNOW ANYTHING ABOUT No. 1?

NOPE.

...IS APPARENTLY HIDING OUT AS ONE OF THE STUDENTS AT THIS SCHOOL.

THE SECOND ONE, WHO RULES OVER THE PRESENT...

WE CAN CONVINCE THEM TO STOP PLAYING PRANKS!

SO IF WE FIND THIS PERSON...

YUP!

AS A STUDENT ...!?

IT'S FROM YOUR CLASS.

YASHIRO.

MY CLASS!?

I SENSE A PRESENCE.

PRESS

YES.

THE KEEPER IS IN HERE.

YOU MEAN...?

YOU MENTIONED A LITTLE WHILE AGO, REMEMBER?

YOUR FRIEND— AOI-CHAN OR AKANE-CHAN...

THE CUTE GIRL WHO'S ALWAYS TELLING YOU ABOUT THE SUPERNATURAL RUMORS.

SHE'S THE ONLY ONE WHO WASN'T AFFECTED BY THE PRANK.

AND DON'T YOU THINK SOMETHING ABOUT THAT IS A LIIIITTLE...

...SUSPICIOUS?

!!

AOI IS...

AOI-CHAN, A SCHOOL MYSTERY? THERE'S NO WAY THAT'S EVEN POSSIBLE!

COME ON!

WHAT ARE YOU SAYING?

WHAT...

HEE HEE!

?

A GIRL'S VOICE...?

HEE HEE HEE!

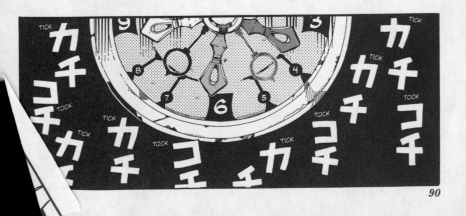

AOI...

OH...

......

U! STARE

HUH?

SORRY, YASHIRO, BUT...

SMIRK

...I'M JUST GONNA LET MYSELF IN FOR A SEC.

ZOOP

FAINT

SHUDDER

SHUDDER

SHUDDER

EEEEP....!?

94

SPOOK 24

THE THREE CLOCK KEEPERS
(PART 2)

AOI'S GONNA THINK I'M A WEIRDO!!

AAAH!

SHAKE

SHAKE

STOPIIIIT!

NENE-CHAN?

THAT MAKES ME SAD...

ARE YOU HIDING SOMETHING FROM ME?

CARESS

OOH LA LA!

KOU-KUN, HURRY—

TURN

IF YOU INSIST ON STAYING QUIET...

KOU-KUN!!?

!?

CLANG

S-SENPAI IS SEDUCING...

I-I'M SORRY...

BLUSH

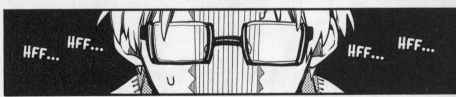

HFF... HFF... HFF... HFF...

HANAKO-KUN—!!!

SENPAI—!!!

!?

WAAAAH!

STOMP STOMP STOMP STOMP

ガッ GRAB

URK!

AAAH!!

べり PUSH

SIGH...

......

ALONE
ぽつん...

FLAIL
ばたばた
FLAIL

Y-
YEAH!

LET'S
GO AFTER
THEM!

IT
HAPPENED
AGAIN...

...I
MISSED MY
CHANCE TO
TELL HER...

HEIGHT: 167 CM—

HE'S MY CLASSMATE, AND AN OLD FRIEND OF AOI'S.

AKANE AOI-KUN!

SHE SAYS THEY LIVE NEXT DOOR TO EACH OTHER.

GLASSES

CHILD-HOOD FRIENDS

CLEVER

AKANE AOI

AOI AKANE

生徒会

ARMBAND: STUDENT COUNCIL

BUUUT.

EVERYONE IN CLASS RELIES ON HIM TOO...

HE'S KIND AND FRIENDLY TO EVERYONE HE MEETS, NO EXCEPTIONS.

I'LL WAIT UNTIL YOU'RE FINISHED.

RIGHT?

AOI'S SUCH A NICE GUY.

YOU FORGOT YOUR PRINT-OUT, DIDN'T YOU?

YOU'RE THE ONLY ONE WHO HASN'T TURNED IT IN, YAMABUKI-KUN.

NORMALLY, HE'S MATURE AND HARD-WORKING.

AND WHENEVER SHE'S INVOLVED, HIS SCREWS GET JUUUST A LITTLE LOOSE...

HE'S HAD A CRUSH ON AOI EVER SINCE THEY WERE LITTLE.

HUH?

OOH... I'VE HEARD ABOUT HIM FROM MY BROTHER.

SIGNS: STUDENT ASSEMBLY / BUDGET MEETING

PRESIDENT, ABOUT THE PROPOSED BUDGETS FOR FIRST SEMESTER.

STUDENT COUNCIL TOP TWO

OH, YES, THAT.

IF I REMEMBER RIGHT...

NII-CHAN'S THE STUDENT BODY PRESIDENT...

...AND THIS GUY'S THE VICE PRESIDENT. AOI-SAN, RIGHT?

TERU MINA-MOTO

WHEN HE SAW HER SWOONING OVER THE BIG BUFF GUYS ON THE SPORTS TEAMS...

...HE STARTED BODY-BUILDING UNTIL HE VOMITED BLOOD.

→ GREAT ATHLETE

WHEN SHE ADMIRED THE STUDENT COUNCIL, HE JOINED UP.

STUDENT COUNCIL VICE PRESIDENT

FOR A BRIGHTER SCHOOL

VOTE FOR ME!

...WHEN AOI-SAN FELL IN LOVE WITH A SUPER-BRAINY GUY, HE STARTED STUDYING LIKE A MADMAN.

SKRTCH SKRTCH

ガ ガ リ

→ TOP OF HIS CLASS

ガ リ SKRTCH

SO HOW MANY CONFESSIONS IS THAT PER DAY?

THAT'S NICE. ♡

I ADORE YOU!!

NOPE!

I LOVE YOU.

100%

NO CAN DO. ♡

MARRY ME.

IT'S A CONSTANT CYCLE OF RECREATING HIMSELF BASED ON THE WORDS AND ACTIONS OF HIS CHILDHOOD FRIEND, CONFESSING HIS LOVE, AND GETTING REJECTED.

CURRENTLY, THE RATIO OF SUCCESSFUL CONFESSION TO REJECTION IS ZERO TO 3,624...

AOI IS A MILD-MANNERED, HARD-WORKING GUY, BUT...

NII-CHAN TOLD ME.

YOU KNOW A LOT ABOUT THIS.

YES, SIR!

SECONDS!

UNDER-STAND?

SO YOU KEEP YOUR DISTANCE, KOU.

...WHEN HIS CHILDHOOD FRIEND IS INVOLVED, HE'LL FLY OFF THE HANDLE AT THE DROP OF A HAT.

JOLT

ゴッ WHAM

AND?

RUMBLE RUMBLE RUMBLE RUMBLE RUMBLE

...YASHIRO-SAN?

WHAT EXACTLY WERE YOU DOING BACK THERE...

OH... NOTHING...

COME TO THINK OF IT, I HAPPENED TO COP A FEEL A FEW MINUTES AGO...

OH!

I WAS JUST, Y'KNOW.

UM, UH...

HUSH
しーん

...AND SHE'S ACTUALLY PRETTY FLAT.

THERE'S, LIKE, THIS MUCH.

WHAP
ばち

BUT WHY!?

YOU EVEN HAVE TO ASK!!?

GIRL OR NOT, YOU'LL PAY FOR THAT!

TAKE YOUR PUNISHMENT !!!

ん!!

WHY?

YOU WANT TO KNOW AO-CHAN'S SECRET?

B... BECAUUUSE...

Shut it!

ISN'T THAT NORMAL?

SMACK

HMMM...

DAMAGE CAUSED BY SCHOOL MYSTERY No.1

I'VE JUST BEEN FEELING LIKE AOI HAS BEEN HIDING SOMETHING FROM ME LATELY......

IT'S BEEN BOTHERING ME SO, SO MUCH, I CAN ONLY SLEEP AT NIGHT NOW...

BECAUSE AOI MIGHT BE ONE OF THE SCHOOL MYSTERIES...

BUT I CAN'T JUST TELL HIM THAT!

YOU WILL?

AOI'S CHILDHOOD FRIEND WOULD BE A GREAT HELP, BUT...

YEAH.

IF THAT'S ALL THIS IS ABOUT, THEN I'LL HELP YOU.

WHAT!?

WELL, ALL RIGHT...

ANYWAY.

I'VE FALLEN IN LOVE... ♥

IF IT'S ANYTHING LIKE THAT...

BUT SHE WON'T TELL ME WHAT IT IS.

SIGH...

YOU'RE RIGHT. AO-CHAN DEFINITELY SEEMS TO BE WORRYING ABOUT SOMETHING LATELY.

IS THAT REALLY WHY?

...WON'T HELP ANY-WAY!

TELLING YOU...

SHE'S SO NOBLE!!

SHE DOESN'T WANT TO WORRY HER LONG-TIME FRIEND...

WAH!

CHILL

...THEN I HAVE TO ELIMINATE THE OFFENDER AS SOON AS POSSIBLE!

生徒会

...I HAVE TO SUPPORT HER, YOU KNOW!?

BECAUSE AS HER CHILDHOOD FRIEND...

AND SO...

THAT'S TRUE!!

YOU'RE EXACTLY RIGHT!!

SCARY!

MUFFLE

もが

YOUR BA—

ONE-DAY ONLY

...IN ORDER TO DISCOVER AOI'S SECRET!

...WE FORMED A TEMPORARY ALLIANCE...

YES, SIR!

SNEAK

HERE'S THE PLAN. WE KEEP WATCH OVER HER, UNDETECTED, UNTIL WE IDENTIFY AO-CHAN'S SECRET.

SO DOMESTIC...

SO CUTE...

SHE'S CLEANING.

SWOON

ON CLEANING DUTY

LET ME BE YOUR MOP!

...AND GETTING CONFESSED TO IN THE PROCESS.

BRUSH BRUSH サッ サッ

115

KASHING

SO FEMININE...

SO CUTE...

SHE'S RAISING PLANTS.

GROW BIG AND STRONG, GUYS! ♡

2

CARING FOR THE PLANTS IN GARDENING CLUB

KASHING

LET ME BE YOUR POTTED PLANT!

...AND GETTING CONFESSED TO IN THE PROCESS.

SO CUTE...

SHE'S WALKING.

TEP TEP

TEP TEP

LIKE A LILY...

3

MOVING FROM POINT A TO POINT B

THAT'S HER FATHER'S JOB!

WHAM

LET ME WALK YOU DOWN THE AISLE!

...AND GETTING CONFESSED TO IN THE PROCESS.

○ ○ ○   I ALWAYS KNEW...   ○ ○ ○

QUEEN OF POPULARITY

KING OF POPULARITY

TOP TWO

AOI

TERU

...BUT SHE REALLY IS RELENTLESSLY POPULAR WITH THE BOYS...

HP
MIN ━━━━━ MAX

GASP

セリ

WHEEZE

セリ GASP

A TRUE GUY MAGNET...!!!

WHEEZE

SHE WENT INTO THE AUDITORIUM.

HUH?

UH, YASHIRO-SENPAI, I THINK YOU'RE MORE—

I THINK THIS IS WHERE THE DRAMA CLUB AND THE SCHOOL BAND HAVE THEIR PERFORMANCES...

AOI'S IN THE GARDENING CLUB...

...SO WHAT WOULD SHE BE DOING HERE...?

CLASP

ガシ

YOU THINK I CAN BE CALM, KOUHAI!!?

PLEASE CALM DOWN, AKANE-SENPAI...

SOMEONE CALLED HER OUT TO TH-TH-THIS EMPTY SPACE...

I BET IT'S A LOVE CONFESSION...

CREAK
ミシ...

...SO BOYS FROM THE WRONG CROWD WOULD OFTEN CALL HER OUT SOMEWHERE WHEN NO ONE ELSE WAS AROUND.

AO-CHAN IS SO CUTE AND NICE...

THEY'D THREATEN HER, TRYING TO FORCE HER TO GO OUT WITH THEM...

THIS STUFF HAS BEEN HAPPENING TO HER EVER SINCE WE WERE KIDS...

SO I'VE BEEN KEEPING AO-CHAN SAFE.

OH, AKANE-KUN! ♡

...BUT I JUST HAPPENED TO BE THERE EVERY TIME.

SO STRONG!

REAL SCARY.

SCARY...

HEH.

ANYWAY.

...EVEN IF SHE'LL NEVER EVER LOOK MY WAY.

I DECIDED I WOULD PROTECT AO-CHAN...

GLANCE GLANCE

キョロ キョロ

STILL...

...BUT HIS LOVE FOR AOI IS THE REAL THING...

HE HAS SOME REALLY CRAZY QUALITIES...

I THINK I'M A LITTLE JEALOUS.

AKANE-KUN...

HANAKO-KUN?

JUST GO WITH IT!

WH-WH-WH-WHAT ARE YOU GONNA DO...?

C'MERE.

ぎゅ
SQUEEZE

...LET'S SAY YOU HAD A POWER YOU WERE HIDING FROM PEOPLE.

WHEN DO YOU THINK YOU WOULD USE IT?

SO, YASHIRO...

WHEN WOULD I...?

...BUT I THINK MOSTLY YOU'D USE IT WHEN THERE WAS A PRESSING NEED.

I'M SURE THERE ARE ALL KINDS OF SITUATIONS...

SWOOSH

FOR EXAMPLE... SOMETHING LIKE THIS.

HUH!?

SNAP

WHOOSH

AOI!!

SNAP

HANAKO-KUN!

!!

AO-CHAN!!

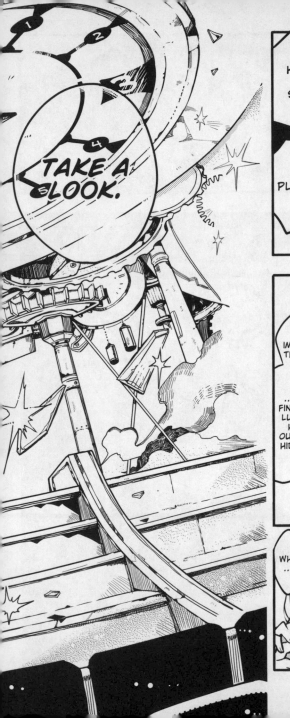

TAKE A LOOK.

HANAKO-KUN, STOP IT!

PLEASE!

THE IMPORTANT THING IS...

...WE FINALLY LURED HIM OUT OF HIDING.

MRGH!

EVERY-THING'S FINE.

WHAT...?

HUSH

OH... KOU-KUN IS STOPPED TOO.

WOW...

THE CHANDELIER...

IT'S STUCK IN MIDAIR...!?

HUSH

PEEK

SO IT'S SAFE TO ASSUME YOUR POWER IS TO STOP TIME.

...I'VE HEARD OF YOU.

CLACK

......

THE THREE CLOCK KEEPERS
(PART 3)

SHATTER

GYA!!

CRASH

KOU-KUN...

!? TURN !?

TURN

WOBBLE

FEH

HUH!?

BADUM

...

THMP

BADUM

RAN OUTTA TIME.

TCH.

DARN IT...

FWAM

!!

BAM

...MAY I TAKE A SWING AT YOU BEFORE WE TALK?

WH-WHOA!

FWISH

NURSE'S OFFICE

I STILL DON'T BELIEVE IT...

IF THEY FIND US HERE, IT'LL CAUSE TROUBLE FOR AO-CHAN...

WE'LL TAKE THIS SOME-WHERE ELSE.

AHEM.

FINE.

YOU'RE ONE OF THE SEVEN MYSTERIES, AKANE-KUN...?

NO NORMAL HUMAN COULD'VE DONE THAT.

HE KNOCKED ME OUT OF YASHIRO EARLIER, REMEMBER?

WHEN DID YOU FIGURE IT OUT?

I WAS GONNA SAVE HER!

OWWW!

IF I WAS WRONG...

KONK

YOU WENT TOO FAR!

OW!

ZZZ... ZZZ... AOI...

WHAP

STRANGLE

OH, I SEE...

MM-HMM.

140

ARE YOU REALLY ONE TO TALK?

BADUM
ドキ

SEE VOLUME 2, CHAPTER 8: THE CONFESSION TREE

THE CONFESSION TREE WAS ABLE TO CONTROL HIM AND EVERYTHING.

I THOUGHT HE WAS JUST A NORMAL BOY...

BUT I HAD NO IDEA.

"VICTIM"?

...I CAN'T BELIEVE YOU'RE A VICTIM JUST LIKE ME.

YASHIRO-SAN...

THAT'S WHAT HAPPENED TO ME TOO.

IT WAS THE DAY OF STUDENT ORIENTATION...

KAMOME ACADEMY MIDDLE SCHOOL

NEW STUDENTS, THIS WAY!

KAMOME

ME?

HE TRICKED YOU INTO FORMING A PACT OR SOMETHING, RIGHT?

STOP!!!

HELLO, BOY.

DO YOU WANT THE POWER TO CONTROL TIME?

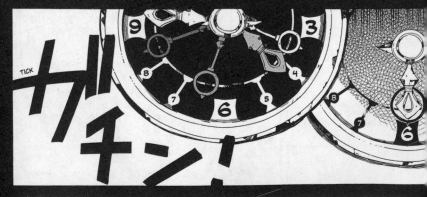

TICK

"DO YOU WANT THE POWER" ...?

I LEARNED LATER...

...THAT THE CLOCK KEEPERS SET THE WHOLE THING UP.

RECRUITMENT: SUCCESS!

ROAR

JUMP

...WHAT A LOAD OF CRAP!!!

SHHGH...

TURN

AND I FELL FOR IT, HOOK, LINE, AND SINKER! DAMMIT!!

THEY WROTE, DIRECTED AND HEADLINED!!

FWAM

FWAM

MY APPEARANCE DOES CHANGE SOME, BUT OTHER THAN THAT, I'M JUST LIKE YASHIRO-SAN.

EXCEPT FOR THIS WATCH, I'M JUST A NORMAL HUMAN BEING.

...I GET TO BE THE OTHER CLOCK KEEPERS' SLAVE.

AS A PART OF SCHOOL MYSTERY No. 1...

MOSTLY CLOCK CLEANING

MY CONTRACT LASTS SIX YEARS.

BASICALLY UNTIL I GRADUATE.

SENPAI...!

FLUSTER

FLUSTER

SHOONK

MASO-CHIST

URK!

HA HA HA!

STILL, SWALLOWING A MERMAID SCALE ON PURPOSE? THAT'S INCREDIBLE, YASHIRO-SAN!

ARE YOU A MASOCHIST?

SO?

THAT DOESN'T MAKE ME HAPPY AT ALL, BUT THANKS...

FWIP

I THINK IT ROCKS!!

I HEAR YOU'RE THE TOP MYSTERY AT THIS SCHOOL, HONORABLE No. 7.

AND ALSO THAT YOU'RE A SLIMY, PERVERTED BRAT.

HE SAID IT TWICE.

SLIMY, PERVERTED BRAT.

STARE

SHOONK

SLIMY

YOU DON'T THINK THAT'S A LITTLE HARSH?

SO WHAT DOES THE SLIMY, PERVERTED BRAT WANT WITH ME?

BARB

BARB

!!

HEY! COME QUICK!!

SOME-BODY!! SOME-BODY COME HELP!!

WAAAAH!

AS FOR WHAT I WANT—

WHAT'S THIS!?

WH—

WHAT'S WRONG!?

DID SOMETHING ELSE HAPPEN!?

DASH

MURMUR

MURMUR

IT'S BAD!

WHAT'S WRONG?

WHOOSH

THEY'VE ALL...

WHA... WHAT'S GOING ON!?

...TURNED INTO OLD PEOPLE ...!!

BABAM
バババン!!

TRASH

OH!

NYOOP

STAIRS SURE ARE MURDER ON MY KNEES.

AAH, OOF...

DAMMIT! AT THIS RATE, OUR SCHOOL'S GONNA TURN INTO AN OLD FOLKS' HOME...

SOME TEA, PLEASE.

WHAT KIND OF CRUEL SUPERNATURAL WOULD...?

EEP!

GRR...!

THAT'S AWFUL... EVEN THE GIRLS...!!

?

HMM!?

OH, I CAN'T QUITE SEE...

YAMA-BUKI...

CREAK Ξ"

CREAK Ξ"

CREAK Ξ"

CREAK

CAN'T WAIT TO POST ABOUT THIS...

HEY, YASHIRO. YO. WHAT'S GOING ON HERE?

HEE HEE!

!!

AAAAAH!! YOU'RE GETTING ALL WRINKLY!!!

YAMA-BUKI-KUN!

DAMMIT! I'VE HAD ENOUGH OF THIS...

SWISH

SKFF

DASH

THERE YOU ARE!!

A CHILD?

SO YOU'RE THE ONES...

...BEHIND THIS SERIES OF DISTURBANCES.

HMPH...

NO, YOU'RE NOT.

...!

AM I WRONG, CLOCK KEEPER?

GOT LOOSE?

MIRAI?

......

"MIRAI" GOT LOOSE.

YES.

YOU KNOW THERE ARE THREE OF US, RIGHT?

1 2 3

ONE OF THE CLOCK KEEPERS...

...CONTROLS THE FUTURE.

APPARENTLY SHE DOESN'T HAVE A NAME, SO I CALL HER MIRAI— WHICH MEANS "FUTURE."

MIRAI

SO THAT'S HOW ALL THAT STUFF HAPPENED...

CATASTROPHE

I'M SURE YOU SAW HER BACK THERE.

MIRAI CAN MOVE TIME FORWARD FOR ANYTHING SHE TOUCHES.

TICK TOCK TICK TOCK TICK TOCK
チワク チワク チワク

...AND THE OLD MAN WAS SUPPOSED TO KEEP HER LOCKED UP IN OUR BOUNDARY.

WE USUALLY MAKE HER WEAR GLOVES SO SHE DOESN'T TOUCH ANYTHING...

I'VE BEEN ORDERED TO CAPTURE HER IMMEDIATELY.

AS IF I WEREN'T BUSY ENOUGH...AND HEY, WHO LET HER ESCAPE IN THE FIRST PLACE...?

MUTTER
ブツ
MUTTER
ブツ
ブツ
MUTTER

WHICH MEANS...

BUT HE'S STILL JUST ANOTHER SUPER-NATURAL.

HA!

THE CLOCK KEEPER WHO CONTROLS THE PAST, KAKO.

OH.

OLD MAN?

THAT ONE ACTUALLY LISTENS TO ME SOME-TIMES.

KAKO

...YOU AND I BOTH WANT TO CATCH THIS "MIRAI."

SFF

WE'LL CATCH HER TOGETHER!

SO LET'S TEAM UP FOR THIS ONE.

OKAY?

I'VE BEEN WONDERING...

TIMID おず

CAN I ASK SOMETHING?

...HATE SUPER-NATURALS?

AKANE-KUN, DO YOU...HATE SUPER-NATURALS?

......

GRIN

GRIN

OF COURSE I HATE THEM.

I DESPISE THEM!

...I THINK IT'S WEIRD YOU'RE ACTUALLY FRIENDS WITH ONE.

IF YOU ASK ME, YASHIRO-SAN...

THAT DOESN'T BOTHER YOU?

WHAT HE DID TO AO-CHAN?

YOU SAW WHAT HE DID BACK THERE.

I THOUGHT YOU AND AO-CHAN WERE BEST FRIENDS?

YEAH. HE'S DEFINITELY SLIMY.

HEY, CAN WE STOP CALLING ME SLIMY?

YUP!

IT HURTS.

HE IS A LITTLE SLIMY...

...BUT WHAT HE DID TO AOI... HE DID IT FOR A REASON...AND I'M SURE HE WASN'T GOING TO HURT HER...

BUT HANAKO-KUN ISN'T BAD.

HE HAD A REASON? OH, REALLY...?

HE'S NOT BAD?

GRAB

BUT...

...YOU KNOW HE'S A MURDERER, RIGHT?

LET ME G—

REFORMED VILLAINS REALLY MAKE ME SICK.

SO WHAT IF THEY'RE GOOD NOW?

DOES THAT ERASE WHAT THEY DID? ...WHAT A JOKE.

THEY DON'T KNOW HOW PRECIOUS IT IS...

THEY DON'T KNOW...

...JUST TO BE ALIVE.

...HOW VALUABLE A HUMAN LIFE IS.

IT'S THE SAME WITH THE OTHER TWO CLOCK KEEPERS.

THESE SUPER-NATURALS DON'T KNOW ANYTHING— NONE OF THEM.

162

FLICK

I WANT TO CATCH MIRAI JUST AS BADLY AS YOU DO.

AND IF YOU'RE WILLING TO WORK WITH ME, I'M GLAD TO HAVE YOU ON THE TEAM.

BUT DON'T WORRY.

EVEN IF YOU ARE A MURDERER.

...HONORABLE No. 7.

HERE'S TO DOING BUSINESS TOGETHER...

...HEH.

...ARE MY FAVORITE KIND.
HERE'S TO DOING BUSINESS TOGETHER.
TO BE CONTINUED IN TOILET-BOUND HANAKO-KUN 6!

TRANSLATION NOTES

Common Honorifics

no honorific: Indicates familiarity or closeness; if used without permission or reason, addressing someone in this manner would constitute an insult.

-san: The Japanese equivalent of Mr./Mrs./Miss. If a situation calls for politeness, this is the fail-safe honorific.

-sama: Conveys great respect; may also indicate that the social status of the speaker is lower than that of the addressee.

-kun: Used most often when referring to boys, this indicates affection or familiarity. Occasionally used by older men among their peers, but it may also be used by anyone referring to a person of lower standing.

-chan: An affectionate honorific indicating familiarity used mostly in reference to girls; also used in reference to cute persons or animals of either gender.

-senpai: A suffix used to address upperclassmen or more experienced coworkers.

-kouhai: The inverse of *senpai*, used to address those who are younger or less experienced.

-sensei: A respectful term for teachers, artists, or high-level professionals.

Page 63

The Japanese "old calendar" is a lunisolar calendar (one that tells both the time of year and the phase of the moon) adopted from China. Japan switched to a Western-style calendar almost a hundred and fifty years ago during the Meiji Era, so it's included on the class calendar more as a piece of trivia than out of any practical reason.

Page 77

Hanako-kun continues to use his free time to play old-fashioned games with the Mokke, breaking out the wooden tops known as *beigoma* for a spin. The goal is to keep your top spinning longer or to knock your opponent's out of bounds, similar to *Beyblades*, for which they served as inspiration.

Page 158

Much like he does with Mirai, Akane calls the keeper in charge of the past "Kako," which literally means "past."

TEACH ME, AKANE-KUN
— HOW YOU USE YOUR POWER —

THE MANGA THAT STARTS ON THE NEXT PAGE IS A ONE-SHOT I DREW BEFORE HANAKO-KUN THAT WAS PUBLISHED IN GFANTASY'S MANGA CONTEST, THE "ABOUT 8 MANGA BATTLE."

PLEASE ENJOY THE HEROICS OF THE OLD AKANE-KUN.

NO WAY!?

THAT'S SCARY!

I HEARD EVEN THE THIRD-YEARS ARE AFRAID OF HIM.

ACK! IT'S YAMA-BUKI.

I'M LEMON YAMABUKI (16), A FIRST-YEAR IN HIGH SCHOOL.

I'VE NEVER BEEN ABLE TO MAKE FRIENDS.

THE MAIN REASON FOR THIS IS THE PERMANENTLY ANGRY EYES I INHERITED FROM MY PARENTS.

DIRECT ATTACK

AND SO I'M EATING LUNCH ALONE ON THE ROOF. AGAIN.

SORRY! MY HAND SLIPPED! ☆

WH-WHAT'S YOUR PROBLEM!?

STOMP
STOMP
STOMP
STOMP
STOMP

BUT COME ON, IF YOU GOT A PROBLEM, YOU SHOULD TELL ME TO MY FACE...

MAN, I WAS SURE I'D BE ABLE TO MAKE A FRIEND ONCE I GOT TO HIGH SCHOOL...

TWO-FACED

RIGHT TO THE POINT

THE REASON FOR THE HOMICIDAL INTENT

LOVE IS BLIND

TEAR DUCT BREAKDOWN

I DIDN'T DO ANYTHING!!

WHAT IS WRONG WITH YOU!?

WHY DOES EVERYBODY I KNOW HAVE TO JUDGE A GUY ON HIS LOOKS...?

WHAT?

WINCE

IT'S YOUR OWN FAULT FOR NOT TRYING TO CHANGE.

DON'T BE NAIVE, YAMABUKI. PEOPLE ARE REALLY 90% LOOKS.

IT'S BECAUSE YOU'RE LIKE THAT...

WEEP.

HE'S CRYING!!!?

IT'S BECAUSE YOU'RE LIKE THAT...

...THAT AO-CHAN FELL IN LOVE WITH YOU!

JUDGING BY APPEARANCES

WHAT?

LET'S JUST PUT THE BAT DOWN FOR A SECOND.

YOU'RE SCARING ME.

THAT'S HOW IT GOES, ISN'T IT? IF THE GIRL YOU LOVE FALLS IN LOVE WITH A HOODLUM, YOUR ONLY OPTION IS TO KILL HIM, RIGHT??

BUT YOU DON'T LOOK LIKE THE REASONABLE TYPE, YAMABUKI.

AND THERE ARE SO MANY UNSAVORY RUMORS ABOUT YOU.

AWWW

YOU'RE SKIPPING SOME IMPORTANT STEPS...FIRST YOU SHOULD TALK IT OUT OR SOMETHING.

MRK!

WHO WOULD HAVE TOLD YOU THAT!?

PSST...

Besides, you're the type who goes out with a girl once, gets tired of her, and dumps her, right?

WERE YOU RAISED IN A BARN!!!?

AM I WRONG?

MY GUT.

YOU JUST HAVE THAT KIND OF FACE.

CHAMELEON AKANE

BUT SHE FALLS IN LOVE SO EASILY.

IT'S NOT LIKE I'M NOT TRYING.

AND I'M THE ONE PERSON SHE'LL NEVER CONSIDER.

スピ
SNIFFLE

WHEN AO-CHAN FELL IN LOVE WITH A MEMBER OF THE BASKET-BALL TEAM, I JOINED UP AND RIPPED THE TITLE OF ACE AWAY FROM HIM.

I BECAME THE CLASS REP AND WAS NICE, EVEN TO PEOPLE LIKE YOU, YAMABUKI.

WHEN SHE FELL IN LOVE WITH A SMART, MILD-MANNERED GENIUS TYPE, I STUDIED TWELVE HOURS A DAY.

← GOT TOP SCORE ON FINALS

...AND HOPE THAT ONE DAY SHE'LL SETTLE AND BE MY GIRLFRIEND.

MAYBE ALL I CAN DO IS KEEP SABOTAGING EVERYONE ELSE'S CHANCES FROM THE SHADOWS...

AND IT STILL DIDN'T WORK.

POOR GUY...

THE TRAUMA OF LOST LOVE

I REALLY DO LOVE AO-CHAN.

C'MON, IT'S NOTHING TO CRY ABOUT.

AND YET...

AO-CHAN!

WILL YOU BE MY BRIDE WHEN WE GROW UP!?

AT AGE SIX...

IF I MARRIED YOU, I'D BE AOI AOI.

SO I CAN'T!

WHEN SHE PUTS IT LIKE THAT, I CAN'T...

I LOVE HOW OUR NAMES MATCH! ♡

......WHAT IF YOU CHANGE YOUR LAST NAME?

THIS IS HOPE-LESS...

REGROUPING

I DIDN'T EXPECT THAT......

...TO FIND OUT YOU DON'T HAVE ANY FRIENDS.

OH, I WAS JUST...SO SURPRISED...

I DON'T KNOW IF ANY OF THEM WOULD STILL BE MY FRIENDS IF THEY KNEW THE REAL ME.

I GET ALONG WITH A LOT OF PEOPLE. BUT IN CLASS, I'M ONLY ACTING NICE.

WELL, YOU BROUGHT THAT ON YOURSELF.

AH-HA-HA.

WELL...

HERE GOES, YAMABUKI!!!

WHAT?

......WHAT!?

FRIENDS

I'VE NEVER TALKED THIS MUCH TO A KID MY OWN AGE BEFORE EITHER.

WHAT A COINCIDENCE.

COME TO THINK OF IT...

...I'VE NEVER TOLD ANYONE ABOUT THIS STUFF BEFORE.

HMMM...

IF AO-CHAN HADN'T FALLEN IN LOVE WITH YOU...

...WE MIGHT'VE BEEN FRIENDS.

ACTUALLY, I DON'T REALLY HAVE ANY FRIENDS I CAN CONFIDE IN...

HUH?

....

DRINK: LOW LEMON

SORRY!

S—

WELL?

LOOM

WHAT'S WITH THE PAUSE? YOU'RE SUPPOSED TO REPLY IMMEDIATELY TO THESE THINGS.

174

BATTLE SCENE

AKANE-KUN...

NOW TO FINISH YOU OFF......

HUH?

I WANTED TO GIVE YOUR BOOK BACK... I HEARD YOU RAN UP TO THE ROOF...

AKANE-KUN...

A... AAA-AO-CHAN !!?

WELL ....

TH—

THIS IS JUST, UM...

I THINK THAT'S A STRETCH FOR ANY IMAGINATION.

B—

BASEBALL! WE WERE PLAYING BASEBALL!

TABOO

I'M TELLING YOU, WE CAN TALK THIS OUT!

WHAT? WHY NOT?

W-WAIT, WAIT! YOU DON'T HAVE TO DO THIS!!!

PUT DOWN THE BAT!

WELL, THAT COULD WORK.

...BUT SHE'S SO CUTE. ARE YOU SURE YOU COULD REJECT HER?

BASICALLY, IF THIS "AO-CHAN" EVER TRIES TO TELL ME SHE LIKES ME, I CAN JUST TURN HER DOWN, RIGHT?

DON'T WORRY!

I'M NOT INTO GIRLS WHO LOOK LIKE PRETEENS!!

HANDWRITING: GLASSES DID IT

YOU MADE ME ANGRY.

WH...... WHY...... ME......?

175

SELF-DESTRUCTION

HE'S NOT EVEN THAT WILD!

N—

YOU'RE SO LUCKY, BEING FRIENDS WITH YAMABUKI-KUN.

NO, I'M NOT!!!

AND, UM, UM...

SHUNK

WHA—? YOU IDIOT!

H-HE SAID YOU LOOK LIKE A PRETEEN!

I HATE YOU! YOU'RE THE WORST, FOUR-EYES!

I DO NOT! STUPID AKANE-KUN!!!

AOI...

WANNA BE FRIENDS?

YOU ARE THE WORST IN SO MANY WAYS, BUT I KIND OF FEEL SORRY FOR YOU.

SHUT UP! I HATE YOU!!!

GOOD GUY

WHAA—!?

BASE-BALL?

YEAH! HE SAID HE WAS SCARED OF CLOSE PLAYS, SO WE WERE PRACTICING!

HOW CAN YOU SAY—!?

THIS ISN'T A FIGHT, OR ME AMBUSHING YOU OR ANYTHING! IS IT, YAMABUKI!?

WE'RE PALS, RIGHT!?

WE'RE FRIENDS, RIGHT?

URK.

EH-EH-HEH.

THAT'S AWESOME!

WHAT!? YOU TWO'RE FRIENDS!!?

YEAH... WE SURE ARE...

176

Toilet-bound
Hanako-Kun

Toilet-bound Hanako-Kun 5

AidaIro

Translation: Alethea Nibley and Athena Nibley
Lettering: Jesse Moriarty

JIBAKU SHONEN HANAKO-KUN Volume 5 ©2017 AidaIro / SQUARE ENIX CO., LTD.
First published in Japan in 2017 by SQUARE ENIX CO., LTD. English translation rights arranged with SQUARE ENIX CO., LTD. and Yen Press, LLC through Tuttle-Mori Agency, Inc.

English translation © 2018 by SQUARE ENIX CO., LTD.

Yen Press
150 West 30th Street, 19th Floor
New York, NY 10001

Visit us at yenpress.com • facebook.com/yenpress • twitter.com/yenpress • yenpress.tumblr.com • instagram.com/yenpress

First Yen Press Print Edition: September 2020
Originally published as an ebook in April 2018 by Yen Press.

Yen Press is an imprint of Yen Press, LLC.
The Yen Press name and logo are trademarks of Yen Press, LLC.

The publisher is not responsible for websites (or their content) that are not owned by the publisher.

Library of Congress Control Number: 2019953610

ISBN: 978-1-9753-1137-7 (paperback)

10 9 8 7 6 5 4 3

BVG

Printed in the United States of America